Conversations with Students
A Princeton Architectural Press series

Other titles in this series

Santiago Calatrava
978-1-56898-325-7

Le Corbusier
978-1-56898-196-3

Louis I. Khan
978-1-56898-149-9

Rem Koolhaas
978-1-88523-202-1

Ian McHarg
978-1-56898-620-3

Mies van der Rohe
978-1-56898-753-8

Frei Otto
978-1-56898-884-9

Paul Rand
978-1-56898-725-5

Peter Smithson
978-1-56898-461-2

Conversations with Paolo Soleri

Paolo Soleri

Edited by Lissa McCullough

Princeton Architectural Press, New York

Princeton Architectural Press
37 East Seventh Street
New York, New York 10003

For a free catalog of books,
call 1-800-722-6657.
Visit our website at www.papress.com.

PAP Editor: Tom Cho
Designer: Bree Anne Apperley

Special thanks to: Sara Bader,
Nick Beatty, Janet Behning,
Nicola Bednarek Brower,
Fannie Bushin, Megan Carey,
Carina Cha, Russell Fernandez,
Jan Haux, Linda Lee, Diane Levinson,
Jennifer Lippert, Gina Morrow,
John Myers, Katharine Myers,
Margaret Rogalski, Dan Simon,
Sara Stemen, Paul Wagner,
and Joseph Weston of
Princeton Architectural Press
—Kevin C. Lippert, publisher

Library of Congress
Cataloging-in-Publication Data
Soleri, Paolo, 1919–
Conversations with Paolo Soleri
/ Paolo Soleri ; edited by Lissa
McCullough. — 1st ed.
p. cm. — (Conversations with
students)
ISBN 978–1–61689-055–1 (alk. paper)
1. Soleri, Paolo, 1919—Interviews.
2. Soleri, Paolo, 1919—Notebooks,
sketchbooks, etc. 3. Architects—
Italy—Interviews. 4. Architectural
design. 5. City planning.
I. McCullough, Lissa. II. Title.
NA9085.S6A35 2012
720.92–dc23
                              2011033412

Contents

Acknowledgments

Gratitude for help with this project goes first of all to an unsung hero, Hanne Sue Kirsch, manager of the Soleri archives at Arcosanti since 2002, whose quiet demeanor belies the tenacity, dedication, and excellence with which she has organized, cataloged, protected, and made available Soleri's work with a long posterity in view. As Soleri would say, bravissima! Also to be thanked is Mary Hoadley, site coordinator of Arcosanti, who for many years has transcribed Soleri's notebook writings into electronic form, making hundreds of pages accessible as they otherwise would not be. This book has benefited from the knowledgeable counsel of Tomiaki Tamura, special projects coordinator at Arcosanti, Youngsoo Kim, and Marco Felici. I am grateful to architect Antonio Fragiacomo for bringing me to meet Soleri at Cosanti in 2005 and providing an excellent initial orientation to his thinking. Finally, this book would not have come to be without the keen interest and support of Paolo Soleri. My thanks to each and all. That this has been an Italian-German-Japanese-Korean-American collaboration is hopefully a sign of times to come.

Lissa McCullough

Soleri: Architecture as Evolutionary Quest

Lissa McCullough

> Where else but in a city does so much latent violence depart
> in peace?
> —Lewis Lapham[1]

Paolo Soleri is best known for his unbuilt projects: his pioneering
conceptual designs of maximally sustainable megapopulation cities,
for which he has coined the term *arcology*, signifying the fusion of
architecture and ecology. At around fifty years old, after many years
of experimenting with hands-on artisanal and building techniques,
drafting bold urban-scale complexes, and defining his philosophical
ideas, Soleri burst into broader public attention with two signal
events: the publication of his groundbreaking book, *Arcology:
The City in the Image of Man* (MIT Press, 1969), and a major
exhibition that showcased his work at the Corcoran Gallery of Art
in Washington, DC, in 1970, attended by more than one hundred
thousand visitors over a period of two months. Book and exhibition
were best taken in tandem, as Soleri's philosophical explorations
and architectural projects were, and still are, equally important for
understanding his lifework as an integrated whole.

In a review of the exhibition, Holcombe M. Austin wrote:

> What they saw were beautiful Lucite models of cities that
> would rise three hundred stories, not slabs or boxes but
> intricate polyhedral structures open to light and air yet
> so ingeniously designed and so masterfully compacted
> that instead of the coast-to-coast sprawl of megalopolis,
> humankind could be housed on a fraction of today's required
> urban acreage. These humanely adequate, ecologically
> justified arcologies, Soleri contends, would save for us what
> remains of unspoiled open land. Indeed, they could reverse
> the current trend and free land for restoration and human
> enjoyment.[2]

A 1958 model created for the
Atlas Cement Corporation of
The Beast, Soleri's first bridge
design, executed while he was
an apprentice to Frank Lloyd
Wright, 1947–48

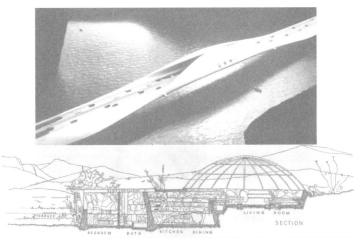

Schematic diagram of Dome
House, constructed in
collaboration with Mark Mills,
1948–49

Exterior of completed Dome
House with Soleri inside, 1949

The gist of arcology is the reversal and inversion of urban sprawl toward the inner limits of compact logistical efficiency. Arcological thinking halts the movement of dispersal that is the essence of sprawl and throws it into reverse—into implosion—retaining but radically shortening all the vital interconnections between people, places, and things. This urban logic shrinks massive cities into intensely interconnected, densely populated, three-dimensional forms on a tightly zoned footprint. Suburbia is curtailed to be more like a tutu than a bridal train or a Milky Way (as seen looking over greater Los Angeles at night, for example).

Arcology is a large black rectangular book brimming with the plans and elevations of such compact cities with populations in the millions. It opens with the puzzling epigraph "This book is about miniaturization." When reading Soleri, one soon realizes that he recommissions certain words to serve his own purposes, and *miniaturization* is one of the most important and difficult. He uses this word to describe the implosive "shrinking" of organic and inorganic processes at any scale. That is, the term does not refer to reducing absolute scale, simply "making things smaller," but rather to maintaining the interactivity, complexity, and circuitry of a system while reducing the amount of space and time required for them to function. The power of miniaturization is exemplified in an insect brain, a microchip, a sonnet, and an urban-scale arcology alike: it occurs when active processes, whether vital, mechanical, electric, or semiotic, are made more complex and intricate, more capable and efficient, by eliminating as much as possible of the needless interposition of space and/or time. According to Soleri's thinking, every event, per se, is spatial and needs space to occur, but how much space an event needs can often be radically reformulated. The shrinking magnitudes of powerful computers demonstrate this superbly.

But just as miniaturization is not a matter of simply making things smaller, neither is Soleri's self-proclaimed minimalism a matter of making things simpler, but rather of making complexity more

streamlined and effective, more frugal, thus enabling it to become
even more complex. In response to Mies van der Rohe's modernist
credo, "Less is more," an arcological minimalism would reply, "Often
less is just less," when less causes a loss of opportunity or potency.
Instead, Soleri's lean credo counsels "Do more with less," which is
the only way to ensure that less is truly more.

Soleri's fundamental point is that life itself is a dynamic
complexity only made possible by miniaturization—superefficient,
hypercomplex interactivity within and between the zillions of cells
in an organism. Because life relies on continual logistical support
and communication at all levels, microscopic and macroscopic,
space-time is an energy sink that organisms constantly labor against:
the distance between oxygen and blood cells is surmounted by

Solimene interior: treelike columns
support multilevel consecutive work
areas that spiral down to the ground-
floor retail space, photo taken 2006

Soleri removing earth-cast ceramic windbell from a mold in the Arizona ground, mid-1950s

Soleri carving pattern into a windbell under the ceramics studio canopy at Cosanti, mid-1950s

the labor of breathing and arterial flow; the distance between the digestive system and sources of nourishment is surmounted by the labor of food production and consumption; the distance between companions and collaborators is surmounted by the labor of transportation; and so on. Shortening these logistical distances relative to scale frees up time and energy formerly required to maintain the system for novel evolutionary achievements that advance new forms of organic complexity. As fewer resources go into maintaining what is, more are available for what might be.

Miniaturization has produced hypercomplex forms of organic interactivity through the course of evolutionary time—a process that Soleri has dubbed the *miniaturization-complexity-duration* principle (MCD). The operation of this principle has generated what he refers to as the *urban effect*, which argues that the advent of cities was not the origin of urban life; to the contrary, it was the urban effect, the organizing of subcellular components and cells into increasingly advanced forms of life, that ultimately impelled the founding of cities. In other words, there is an evolutionary continuity between the hypercomplex, interactive urban structure of molecular organisms and the hypercomplex, interactive urban structure of the *hyperorganism* that is the city, the apex of human culture and civilization. Urban life in all its forms, from cellular to civilizational, is a product of MCD in action.

Tracing MCD as the evolutionary engine of life that generates the increasingly complex formations of the urban effect over time, Soleri extrapolates that cities are the sine qua non of continuing human evolutionary development. Suburban development, by contrast, is a weakening and parasitic trend. He characterizes suburbanism as the *metastasis of the city* into a planetary hermitage, producing segregation, isolation, and intensified privatization, thereby effecting a counterevolutionary dissipation of creative energy and purpose. Contrary to miniaturization, *gigantism* is dynamically and expensively pursued by the automobile-defined suburb, with its ever-widening roadways, ever-creeping acres of parking lots, ever-ballooning McMansions and big-box stores, and its ever-increasing, desperate, and deadly addiction to petroleum.

Rem Koolhaas has coined the term *junkspace* to describe this "disappearance of architecture in the twentieth century," as he characterizes it. He sings the dispraises of incoherence:

> Junkspace looks as if a hurricane has rearranged a previously ordered condition, but that impression is misleading—it was never coherent and never aspired to be…it exploits any invention that enables expansion.[3]

To accept this negative analysis of gigantism and incoherent expansionism is also to recognize that attempts to reform it are counterproductive, only tending to reinforce dysfunctional urban forms and increase overall waste. Soleri has devised the term *a better kind of wrongness* to describe this kind of improvement of an inherently dysfunctional system ("green" cars are a prime example, in his view). Firmly set against the idea of reform,

Soleri accents the need for *reformulation*. There is an urgency to radically rethink and reconfigure cities to embody logistical coherence, a countergigantism—a *lean alternative*—by applying to urban forms the practice of frugality as a creative virtue, a virtue that is at the very origins of life.

Cities cannot achieve life-enhancing functionality and grace on an urban scale without emphasizing the material logic that is etymologically implied in "logistics" at the very core of every design. As urban planner Edmund N. Bacon has expressed this:

> If the architect deals primarily in form, the chance of his work being modified or destroyed in future years is relatively great. If the architect deals with movement systems, if they are well conceived in relation to the larger systems of movement, and if they are rendered articulate, the chances of their survival, and indeed of their strengthening and extension over time, are very good indeed, even if the structures along them are torn down and rebuilt.[4]

Recognizing this principle in full, Soleri's Lean Linear Arterial City proposal conceives the city itself as a transportation corridor. Static elaborations are imagined to come and go as communities and cultures change, while the arterial logistical routes and skeletal passive-energy structures remain the permanent urban core.

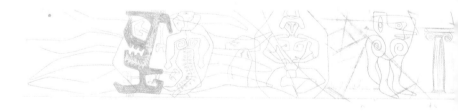

The city is primarily imagined in terms of motion and energy generation, secondarily in terms of static elements.

But Soleri's commitment to the city is not a merely pragmatic concern for housing—or "storaging," to borrow his own word—a huge population. At its heart, arcology implies a humanism. Human beings have complex emotional, intellectual, and existential needs that only the realm of cultural creation can address and assuage. They cannot live packed into colonies patterned on beehives or termite hills; the qualities of the city must respond and correspond to the profounder human needs. *Arcology*'s humanistic subtitle, *The City in the Image of Man*, is a reminder that human beings are highly individuated *personae* whose vital needs are as much cultural as they are physical. A person can die of meaninglessness as readily as he or she can die of starvation. It follows that the "sustainability" of urban formations implies more than healthy ecosystems. Sustainable cities must also address questions of justice and equity, tolerance and compassion, and opportunities to grow and flourish through exposure to beauty as much as possible and to misery, degradation, and directionless cultural inertia as little as possible.

Urban structures are essentially a means of bringing individuals together into a complex cooperative life—an urban life with potentials far transcending the tribal—and we thereby civilize *ourselves*. Civilization is epitomized in the civilized person,

Sketch depicting the *History of Man* beginning from the sun, late 1950s

Soleri's brother Luciano working in covered outdoor area of Cosanti ceramics workshop, 1960s

Swimming pool at Cosanti, with earth-cast canopy supported by recycled telephone poles, ca. 1970

Cosanti ceramics canopy, with circular windows of Soleri drafting studio at left, hanging windbell assemblies at center, and bell molds below, photo taken 2007

in the human element and attitude, not in buildings and cultural products per se. How we live together—in what spirit and with what intention—defines the heart of civility. Hence, for Soleri, sustainable high-density cities are not an end in themselves but a means to civilizing and transforming ourselves. The city is an evolutionary instrument, an advanced technology for catalyzing human self-creation and self-transcendence through collective social venture; it is a hyperorganism, evolving toward new forms by putting the *we* before the *me*, while respecting and cultivating the individual persona as such.

If human "spirit" as embodied in the persona is a vital resource for nurturing new, more promising ways of being human, then the suburban dissipation and diaspora, characterized as "the geography of nowhere" by James Howard Kunstler, is an expense of spirit we can little afford. The sterility of suburbia—this "triumph of mass merchandizing over civilization," in Kunstler's words—is symbolized in the very cul-de-sac that is its preferred expression.[5] Whereas the essential intent of an arcology is to maximize connectivity in service of life, the cul-de-sac exemplifies detachment and disconnection, a dead end without outlet or further purpose.

Only an arcology can begin to exemplify a fully human, fully humane city by ingathering all the complexities of the "human genome"—as Soleri often refers to bioculturally evolving humanity—and guiding it toward unpredictable novel creations as evolution continues. Architecture at its best, in his view, strives toward increasing coherence and transcendence, which implies a built environment geared toward cooperation, tolerance, benevolence, and beauty. It creates structures in pursuit of what Soleri calls *esthequity*—an evolutionary quest for moral-esthetic fulfillment that is engaged in by all.

Soleri views human potential in light of five million years of hominid evolution: every human being, as an instantiation of the human genome, embodies a compendium of ambiguous qualities ranging from the opportunistic, aggressive, and greedy to the altruistic, compassionate, and cooperative. He employs binomial nomenclature to emphasize specific facets of this human potential, such as *Homo faber* (man who fabricates things), *Homo rapax* (rapacious man), and *Homo amor* (man who is loving). When he uses the term *Homo sapiens*, for example, he intends to emphasize the creative powers of human intelligence (in Latin *sapiens* means knowing, wise).

In Soleri's thinking, the self-disciplining values and virtues that are called upon to formulate a sustainable, complex, life-enhancing, humane city are the very ones that are most essential to take us to the next level of being human, living together in a single, now-unified world. Only by learning to live together more and more successfully will the human genome enact its fuller potential as a self-creating phenomenon. When Shakespeare wrote, "What a piece of work is a man, how noble in reason, how infinite in faculties, in form and moving how express and admirable, in action how like an angel, in apprehension how like a god," he enumerated the wealth of capacities that we disappoint with the present condition of global civilization.[6] Though perfection is not of this world, we are unjustifiably far from trying for it.

And there is no point in waiting for a god to save us. We must work. We must think, levering ourselves out of this "Bermuda Triangle of concepts," as Koolhaas has dubbed our era of architectural-intellectual incoherence.[7] The minimalism implied by Occam's razor, also known as the *lex parsimoniae*, has for Soleri eliminated every justification for speaking of God or gods. Therefore whenever he speaks of "religion," he voids and reformulates the word. He obliterates every definition of religion as our common language defines it. In its place he puts *religare* (Latin for "to bond together"), the linking and bonding that is the dynamically interactive essence of life—at the subatomic level, the molecular level, the organismic level, and the hyperorganismic level. *Volition*, as Soleri defines it, is the motive force at work in *religare*; it is the driving eros toward connectivity that is the condition of the possibility of life. Religion and volition, which function inextricably in tandem, form a will or drive to bond, interact, and self-organize, transcending the existing state of things with novel forms of interconnectivity and complexity, thus making possible the creation of every urban phenomenon ranging from the microorganism to the city.

Soleri's ultimate concern is with cosmic evolution and the place of planet Earth within it: especially the miracle of life on Earth and the advent of *Homo sapiens* within the massively vaster, colder, older, and utterly inhospitable cosmic reality. As a fundamental architectural thinker, Soleri conceives the entire universe as a molten, violent, unconscious architecture: it is *space in metamorphosis*— an infinitely complex reality in process of furiously generating and creating itself. The concept of *self-creation* receives emphasis in his later writings to supplant the defunct notion of creation by God, and his repeated references to the big bang acknowledge the source of all of this churning, self-generating, self-creating mystery. The fact that life—and human self-conscious life in particular—has emerged out of the self-generating cosmic laboratory is cause for bottomless wonder and celebration, which he evokes with the term originally coined by Rudolf Otto to describe the utmost religious experience: *mysterium tremendum*. Soleri sees extraordinary reason for optimism in the fact that there is life, that life has evolved from a situation of nonlife, seemingly against all odds—perhaps the only form of optimism that is cosmically justified.

What makes Soleri's thinking as an architect singular is his concern for cosmic and planetary coherence, a coherence that ultimately demands that the urban effect be our counsel; that waste be minimized because frugality is a life-creating virtue and potentiating grace; that equity, tolerance, and compassion be maximized to enhance the interactive cooperation that is the "religious" origin of life; and that humans become more conscious of their powers as self-creating matter–cum–evolving conscious mind or "spirit." Our cities should be compact, cooperative, multifunctional, waste-minimizing environments that concentrate creative energies instead of disintegrating and degrading them in the energy sink of sprawl, gigantism, auto-isolation, auto-enclosure, "hermitage" culture, inequity, bigotry, and squalor, while also leaving as much of the natural world as possible free from suburban and exurban encroachment.

Despite its seeming idealism, this lean thinking is a hypothetical realism, offering practical proposals to contend with the world's most urgent urban-infrastructural, environmental, and ethical problems. It addresses global climate change and reduction of oil dependence; it embraces frugality and an ethic of radically reduced consumption leading to more equitable sharing of all the goods of life; it confronts issues of land waste, habitat encroachment (resulting in species extinction), suburban sprawl, and urban renewal; and it recommends wiser approaches to agricultural production and water conservation.

As Marco Felici's essay in this book outlines, the emerging Soleri of 1970, seemingly a visionary, was in fact a pioneer. Still today, with the Lean Linear Arterial City, he is formulating working models for transforming societal systems through the lean alternative, as Youngsoo Kim's essay argues, while also raising our sights to an expansive and exhilarating evolutionary perspective.

Soleri with a model of his Bow Bridge design and windbells in the North Studio, now the Cosanti Gift Gallery, late 1960s

Soleri at Cosanti with earth-cast plaster model of Double Cantilever Bridge, with Single Cantilever Bridge model in the background, ca. 1963

The global human population recently surpassed seven billion, a massive proportion of whom are slum dwellers living under hazardous conditions, while 25 percent of our fellow mammal species are threatened with extinction. Most schools of architecture are only beginning to wake up to this real-world context of all building design and construction today. To become truly realistic, architecture needs to be reformulated from the twenty-first century forward as a planetary ethics in search of urban forms adequate to its ethical mandate. This means moving away from single-building fetishism: a shortsighted preoccupation with formal esthetic design challenges that are divorced from larger civilizational, ethical, and environmental concerns. For almost half a century, Soleri's insistent lean proposal has been to concentrate human habitation into densely integrated arcologies that radically reverse automobile gigantism and urban metastasis in favor of walking, cycling, and train transportation, sparing the immediately surrounding agricultural lands and natural habitat for other species—and the joyful re-creation of our own. As compared to 1970, there is even greater urgency today that this call to coherence be heard.

1   Lewis H. Lapham, "City Light," *Lapham's Quarterly*, Fall 2010, 4, http://www.laphamsquarterly.org/preamble/city-light.php.

2   Holcombe M. Austin, review of an exhibition by Paolo Soleri at the Corcoran Gallery of Art, Washington, DC, *Journal of Aesthetics and Art Criticism* 33, no. 1 (1974): 115–16.

3   Rem Koolhaas, "Junkspace," in *Constructing a New Agenda: Architectural Theory 1993–2009*, ed. A. Krista Sykes (New York: Princeton Architectural Press, 2010), 137–38.

4   Edmund N. Bacon, *Design of Cities*, rev. ed. (New York: Viking, 1974), 306.

5   James Howard Kunstler, *The Geography of Nowhere: The Rise and Decline of America's Man-Made Landscape* (New York: Simon & Schuster, 1993), 166. The urban historian Lewis Mumford voiced a comparable judgment thirty years earlier: "Life for the everyday American, under a compulsive economy of expansion, is essentially a gadget-ridden, goods-stuffed emptiness puffed up for profit" (Lewis Mumford, *The City in History: Its Origins, Its Transformations, and Its Prospect* [New York: Harcourt, Brace & World, 1961], 226).

6   William Shakespeare, *Hamlet*, act 2, scene 2, lines 303–8.

7   Koolhaas, "Junkspace," 137.

Writings from Soleri's Notebooks

Editor's note: Since his early thirties, Paolo Soleri has recorded philosophical reflections almost daily in his notebooks and sketchbooks. The following excerpts have been selected primarily from his most recent notebooks (2004–2011), with occasional borrowings from older sources. The selection is intended to accent topics of particular interest to architects and urban planners while also conveying a handful of Soleri's core philosophical ideas that go far beyond architectural design per se. Many key terms that Soleri uses in a distinctive sense are outlined in the introduction as an aid to the reader. My notes are added in brackets.

Autobiographical Musings

I am trying to define the *whatness* of things by way of their *howness*. The howness of space metamorphosis, that is the gist of becoming, of reality. *How* after *how* after *how*, and here we are, glamorized hydrogen.

I am routine oriented. Passion would make me a wreck. Reality (what is it?) is a monstrous and relentless muse seizing upon the persona!

I don't have an ideology. I work on the basis of evolutionary guidelines because seven billion personas are in terrible danger. The past of human habitat is an open book of pros and cons. Self-creation is rainbowlike, consisting of all colors.

My "falling in love" with nature and the period of such incantation spanned from age four to approximately eighteen, the age when culture begins to elbow nature to one side. That was the Aquarian extent of my concern in the 1920s and 30s. I moved from the ape culture of Tarzan to the ambiguous, inspiring, hermetic culture of books, music, painting, sculpture, architecture, and the forays of the mind into the domain of matter. The apparent stillness of things invokes arcadian landscapes in which body and mind can dwell; but it is belied by an immensely dynamic turbulence that is the substratum to the apparent quiet—subatomic, atomic, molecular, cellular, organismic, and macrobiological. Turbulences are the domain of miniaturization-complexity-duration [see editor's introduction for a summary of this concept].

I never "practiced architecture." The Solimene project came about while I was learning some ceramics techniques at the factory in Vietri sul Mare on the Amalfi Coast. In planning and architecture, I have mostly dealt with simulation, that is, modeling that rarely entered the

A detailed proto-Arcosanti hand
drawing executed for Arcology
by Soleri studios, 1968

construction phase. For years I have also been "playing" in
the hypothesis domain—the "what if?" In that field, the
modeling approach has a different character. It deals with
notions of finality, of purpose, that daily routine and an
immediate coherence ignore.

The modeling phase, searching the *how* for a *what*
shrouded by ignorance, has given way to a *why* trying to
emerge. If we have access to the *what* via the meanderings
of howness, we could perhaps decide to stop at the gate of
the *why,* because beyond that gate is naught, or a strong
dosage of impotence. Inadequacy is the hovering plague:
"You are a slab of meat nourished by ignorance!"

Like little Michelangelo's chiseling out of David or Moses or the Virgin from mute, informal white stuff in the despairing silence everywhere, so I am trying to put to use my innocent model of a minimalist position: *space is it*. No dualistic bivalence of Creator and creature.

Why of all things is space "privileged"? Anything—large or small, newborn or old, animated or inanimate—is in, and only in, space; spatiality is the sine qua non of reality. Only the past is spaceless, unless the past itself needs spatial storage, requiring a spatial presence.

Each brain is the storage of the past. When needed, memory, a space geometry, retrieves the specific fragment of the past to become an active partaker in the present, the now. The past is ingrained in the texture of becoming. That is why, for instance, we can date the age of objects, mineral and organic. A better equipped *Homo sapiens* will uncover more of the "presents" buried in the past and act them out in the process of self-creation.

If cavorting space is all there is, does it critically matter if it is the warped space of Einstein or any other kind? Geometries are geometries are geometries.... I have been naming it *il mistero tremendo* [Italian for *mysterium tremendum*; see introduction]. That does not refer solely to my huffing and puffing around our hermetic, inscrutable reality, but also to the comedic exertion of hominids: breast-beating in

Soleri in May 1971

the face of a cosmic nothingness. But then, if presence is incorruptible—that is, eternal—then…? The done cannot be undone; that is, the done is eternal.

Are then the gods holding the strings controlling all possible pasts of space—already contextualized (already past) or in line to become so (predestined)? Are the infinite boredoms of déjà vu behind us, and the not-yet-contextualized waiting in line for contextualization ahead?

Self-creation is the singing alternative. That is why "the future" is a bleak notion. The gods are escape routes to nowhere.

What I call the presence of fate can be seen as a powerful determinant lodged in the past, the past that is the product of self-creating becoming. Self-creation can be generous; it is able to renounce the bleak inclination toward idolatry without resorting to further falsifications. It contends instead that labels of all kinds can be monstrous falsifications.

Everything has two sides, the positive and the negative. The "limbo hours"—for me between 2:00 a.m. and 6:00 a.m.—are the surfacing of the negative. It comes in isolation or it might cascade over you. But the true limbo is when positive and negative blur into the indifferent and the persona disappears. What is left is a sea of indefinable anguish.

So here I am, small, limited, and defenseless in my reformulatory garments, grateful to my associates and friends.

My new target? The old target. Coherence for one and all.

Orchid and Forest

Within the architectural profession, I distinguish between the *form givers*, with the "orchids" they often produce, and the *forest architects*. Given the number of people in need of shelter, we require the equivalent of the forest, that is, cities coherently designed. In the urban forest, orchids are welcomed as orchids might be welcomed in the organic forest.

The architect who is mainly dedicated to creating beautiful orchids for an elite minority and public structures like airports, corporate buildings, libraries, museums, etc., is less engaged in producing the forests (cities) that seven billion people need. I am engaged in the forest feasibility not through reforming existing malfeasances but through the total reformulation of habitat itself.

The habitat imperative of our time designates the urban forest as primary. As much as we may love architectural orchids—and architects beg and pray for the chance to author at least one in their career—orchids do not have an autonomous, rich life. They border on parasitism.
The urban forest is where the urban effect flourishes.

Panorama of Arcosanti in
process, with a crane indicating
that it remains an ongoing
construction site, 1970–present

For the body-brain of *Homo sapiens,* the city is the urban forest. Cities have for millennia authored civilizations. To forget this might be our undoing. When seven billion people need shelter, orchids will not do; billions of mediocre orchids would become the killing field of man's "spirit."

We are prototyping nutcrackers, sewing machines, artificial hearts, refineries, submarines, space probes, telephones, vaccines, computing machines, soup cans, chairs, soaps, electric razors—you name it. For all, trial and error have led to success, when success has come. This country spends billions of dollars on a super bomber that never reaches the assembly line and billions in space probes going nowhere. We have been prototyping habitat for thousands of years, but in taking the most complicated and most complex problem of all—the production of culture inside habitat—we have been less than coherent.

We must try and try again, but we must be more focused and less shortsighted. At stake are the lives of billions of people and a considerate symbiosis with the life that made and makes us: the biosphere. We need urban laboratories as a place to prototype. Haphazardness on the

Model of Arcosanti 5000 (for 5,000 inhabitants): the "Old Town" existing construction is nestled inside in gray with the curving vaults visible at its center, 2005

basis of "I do what I like if I can get away with it" is inching closer and closer to irresponsibility in the name of freedom, democracy, happiness, and utopia (the great fiction!).

The common "tragedy of the commons" [Garrett Hardin's term] has two heads. The first, everybody is responsible, leading to paradise on Earth—a pure utopian delusion, cruel. The second, everybody is responsible, and therefore nobody is—the most powdery form of anarchy (formlessness), violence, entropic hell. In the first, greed vanishes—one of the delusions. In the second, greed triumphs—part of "self-expression."

The design practice of today is an endorsement and implementation of the consumerist icon. It is in fact the harboring of limitless consumerist anxiety, taking us deeper and deeper into the "paradise" of materialism. One of the features of materialism is indifference toward equity. Admiring as I do the skill, cleverness, and elegance of today's design practitioners, I am disturbed by the virtuality of their virtuosity. Are we all out of touch?

Responsibility of the Architectural Profession

"Great architecture" is part of the esthetic world being generated by *Homo faber–Homo sapiens*. While a truly traumatic transformation is occurring through the evolution of science and technology, the architectural profession has not as yet shown a deep grasp of its determinant position within the "newness of the new." The imaginative freedom of the planner and architect entering the "flamboyant age" is formalistically exciting, often splendiferous, but its content is vitiated by incoherence vis-à-vis the enormous responsibility of the architect as the maker of habitat for a civilizing seven billion people.

Architects and interior designers are scenographers (set designers); they are in the theater business. If there were to be progress, the millions of designers throughout the world should stop and think, "If my dedication is *really* my contribution to materialism, it would be wise for me to take a sabbatical in the Congo, in North Korea, in the butcheries so popular here and there, to find out about the condition of humankind, try a little harder to discover why I am a mix of grace and disgrace. To wise up a little."

Our responsibilities as habitat makers are great. Eventually every single one of us will have to respond to his or her conscience. Will we be makers or breakers of a sustainable civilization on our planet?

My engagement in environmental concerns for over forty years as an architect has been a lonely experience. I maintain that intervening in the effect while ignoring the causes is a futile and often dishonest battle. It tends to confirm my thesis that the improvement of a wrong thing resolves itself into an even more wrong "solution": this is what I call a better kind of wrongness. In such a case, improvement leads from bad to worse because the "improvements" deliver temporary amelioration and only lead eventually to a more protracted and chaotic breakup. The habitat of speculators, planners, architects, and builders is a classic case, and the bleakness of an unsustainable urban sprawl is the effect.

The major emphasis in design of habitat today is the exurban metastasis, which has been aggressively promoted by the hyperconsumption industry in its marketing of enticing model homes. The metastasis of the city, in the form of suburban and exurban developments, the most pernicious of our intrusions in the environment, is the industry of a better kind of wrongness pursued on a planetary scale. We, along with the whole of life, suffer from this opaqueness.

But while pursuing a better kind of wrongness, architecture is rewarded with comfort and status, enticed by dynamism and synergy. This style of architecture owes its pervasiveness to the comfort zone it delivers by cultivating the consumerist habits of users. Habituated consumers are always in the market for a better home appliance, a better noisemaker, a better gadget to add to yesterday's gadgets to fill spaces, homes, closets, attics, cellars, garages, parking lots, and eventually dumping grounds.

We architects remain provincial and bigoted because the planetary and cosmic sense of the exhilarating upheaval of our time has yet to register its full impact within the profession. My insistence on the disparity between mere reform and total reformulation is a distinction of a critical nature. Historically, architecture has gone through a series of reformations, stylistic developments, interpolated by reformulations of content and of structural-technical novelties.

Inequities are universally present, more or less, in all societies to some degree, and it is becoming quite clear that the materialism favored—if not generated—by a consumerism that knows no bounds is not going to improve the dignity and well-being of most of us. A wrong approach to food and a wrong approach to shelter spell pain and suffering. That is why agriculture and city planning are the areas where a better kind of wrongness spells catastrophe.

Either part of the solution, or part of the problem! That is the problematic of planning and architecture. To my knowledge, the state of the art is part of the problem.

Designers, planners, and architects are mostly intent on carrying forward the history of fashion where they can inscribe their personality. Some are able to transcend the fashion world and become reformulators, by which they move from fashion to evolution; the habitat of *Homo sapiens sapiens* is about its collective cultural nexus acting evolutionarily (not only fashionably).

Given the nature of the species—rational, passionate, and personal in varying degrees—our connection with the past can be preponderantly informational and statistical or preponderantly emotive, depending on the intellectual and passionate charges of the person. What is not helpful is ignorance about our ancestry, recent and remote. The greater the ignorance of what has made us, the greater the incoherence of our work, its segregation from the tide of becoming.

In the urban planning and architectural profession, the longer the history embraced from the past, and the longer the anticipation of things to come, the greater the access to a knowledgeable and serviceable present. That requires knowledge infused in the architectural subject.

Lean Linear Arterial City: view of Inner Park from a bridge, generated from a 3-D computer model made for Beijing Center for the Arts exhibition, 2010

The City as Hyperorganism

Two worlds apart—biosphere and homosphere—are
contained within one single process: the living process.
Architecture refers to the homosphere. As the organic is
not architectural so architecture cannot ever be organic.
The brain sees to that. It filters that which impacts our
senses into that which is essentially, intellectually *Homo
sapiens*. The integrated city module considered as "organism"
is necessarily nonorganic because it is the work of the
discriminatory brain; it is a post- or hyperorganism
webbed with human intelligence. I have never spoken
of architecture as organic. There is no such thing. We
need to watch out; language is often sloganeering.

There is the cosmic engine of no intent, poised at
the edge of presence according to probabilistic quantum
rules. There is the biosphere engine nested in the cosmic
engine under Darwinian rules of innocence. There is the
homosphere engine nested within the biosphere engine
at the point of loss of innocence—the price paid by *Homo
sapiens* for self-awareness and the marvels it is self-creating
toward. (Self-awareness is never innocent; it "knows"
too much.)

It is not right to say that the city is like an organism,
but it is perhaps more telling and normatively useful to say
that the city is a hyperorganism; that is to say it has to find
whatever accommodation it might desire not in letting go
of self-control and self-discipline but instead introducing
them in their self-transcending dimension. Rightly so, if
we truly believe that the self-creational character of
becoming is for real. The art of living belongs to such a
self-transcending dimension.

An organism is under the rule of subordination, that
is, the discipline necessary to maintain a hierarchy of

participation among its organs. A city is under the rule of insubordination, that is, the unwillingness to accept the hierarchies needed to structure the performance of the system. The self-control of the organism is not available to the city. Two alternatives: either the city succeeds in being the transcendence of the organism's rigor—the city as a hyperorganism; or the city winds up a creature of chaos— a state that can advance in becoming only if it transcends its own nature, into hyperchaos.

It is a question of genes versus memes. An organism is under the dictate of its own genes. The genes of the palm tree have been its disciplinarian for millions of years— same genes, same tree. A city formulates itself under the collective demands of its memes, in constant evolution and devolution. In the tree, there is the process of the young seedling inescapably guided toward being the palm tree and only the palm tree. The "comfort" available to the palm tree,

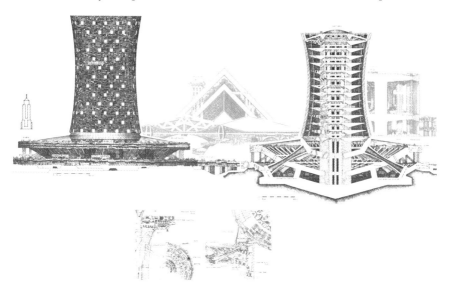

A page from *Arcology* depicting Babel IID arcology, 1969

courtesy of its genetic matrix, is not afforded to the city, captive as it is of its own mercurial memes.

The metastasis of the city, the preference for hermit pseudoculture, and the predilection for the car have succeeded in designing the sterile automobile landscapes of suburbia. The qualifications of hermitage culture are bigness, flatness, isolation, logistical crippling, land destruction, soil decay, aquifer degradation, quarantine of forests, pollution, and, inevitably, materialism— a biblical-scale catastrophe.

The metastasis of the city that has generated suburbia and exurbia is soon to become a planetary phenomenon to be serviced by six billion cars, replaced every five to six years. Ignoring this, green intentions only lead to brown results. Any "green" improvement increases the appetite of the market-hungry consumer. The "greener" the car becomes, the more cars will hit the road, until the American dream of one car per person will be a fact leading to additional browning of biosphere and culture.

We need to rethink the relationship between persona and automobile, which is more and more a form of idolatry of persona for the car, and the almost irresolvable fact that where planning is designed by the car and for the car (that is, grids of roads and streets), there is no resolution in sight. We are dealing with gigantism, rendering our habitat no longer on a human scale. Reformations are showing their inability to correct a system intrinsically wrong. What is in order is a reformulation, a radical reordering of our collective priorities. The first step would be to recognize that what is imperative in the organism is the constant necessity of serving the flesh, which the life-giving and cleansing reticulum of arteries and veins superbly do. The emulation of the performance of the artery-vein is imperative for the creational process.

Gigantism is a pathology of performance.

Civilization and culture beg for excellence and sophistication. Under the demand for such critical and creational conditions, the city, and only the city, delivers. Given that life is in the thick of things, let's find human coherence in this fact. History suggests that only the city does that.

The wisest and most prudent architects and planners point to the city not as an organism but as a potpourri of one kind or another. Their fault might lie in ignoring the makeup of organisms, their genesis, and their possible transcendence into the hyperorganism composed of a thousand or a million body-brains: the city. The termite hill is a non-self-aware hyperorganism. The city is, or could be, a self-aware hyperorganism. An immense difference.

In architecture, purposeful spaces are the objectives and the consequences of matter made more orderly and more ephemeral—Gothic cathedrals, crystal palaces—that is, matter moving in the direction of mind. Our towns and cities are crude, infantile, unwise, arrogant specimens of an urban effect within which a willed destiny could encompass the whole of reality.

Soleri with styrofoam model of
Babelnoah arcology, 1967

The Urban Effect

The pulse of geometry as self-creating reality: the lean (minimalist) hypothesis. The "miracles" reality seems to be performing effortlessly, routinely, here and there in its own space immensity are coming about in the nanogeometry and nanobiogeometry of its metamorphosing. A furious metamorphosing occurring at trillions of pulses per second, a speed we cannot begin to grasp since we are made by it.

Life on this planet originates and evolves courtesy of complexity and miniaturization that combine in a critical mass of such intensity that volition and "religion" (bonding) are triggered within the cellular envelopes we call organisms. I call this stupendous and stupefying event the urban effect. Evolution testifies to the indispensability and power of the urban effect.

The urban effect might be relatively simple as in bacteria or viruses, or it might be unbelievably complex as in the human species. It might be a relatively simple association of elementary organisms as the coral reef or a complex association of complex organisms as in a human city, but the underlying nature of all these events is the same—the resonance (sufferance) of the single cell or individual with the whole and vice versa. That is the nature of crowding. We *are* "crowding" to the most intense degree and in the best sense of the term.

The urban effect is, then, proposed as the recurring and imperative effect running through evolution from the very early unicellular organism onward, and it is characterized with ever-growing force by the implosion of a relatively indifferent milieu—the nonliving universe—into discrete, distinguishably complex, and necessarily miniaturized systems. Therefore the city that promises an access into the "future" must be that habitat that abides by the imperative of MCD.

The urban effect is generated by miniaturization-complexity-duration. The evolution of the urban effect is the best example of the synergy that the MCD paradigm is proposing. All organisms are per se different stages of the urban effect and its bonding power, its power of *religare* (to bond together). The "religion" of MCD is pointing toward the "city of light" that throughout history has been emblematic of the highest of all transfigurations, matter transfigured into mind.

Religare is innate to organism. It is the synergistic bonding of stardust (atomic and subatomic) in close collective proximity (miniaturization). From this tightly woven interaction, complexity emerges. Miniaturization-complexity at a ceiling of "exasperation" surmounts the nanotechnological bond and produces the supreme novelty of volition: nano-*bio*-technology, nesting between micro- and megatechnology.

What distinguishes a system that is alive from one that is not? I would answer volition-religion. In the system, the cells develop new internal stress-alterations (via changing space geometries) unique to the system, a volitional pattern. For this to succeed the cohesion among the parts has to have an implosive growth, a powerful bonding, a "religious" bonding. The two new sequences—volition and religion—in constant turmoil and reciprocal enhancements are life.

When, a remote time ago, volition and *religare* bumped into each other, that is, found significance together, life was triggered. Here we are, the progeny of that collision.

In the context of things (reality), life is a deviance. To demonstrate and confirm its validity, life needs to bridle reality, of which it is a deviance, to the extent of remaking reality into its own image: a self-willed presence.

Where there is volition, there is religion! The two are inseparable and extraordinary. See the evolution of a

Arcosanti North and South
Vaults, an eleven-meter-high
communal space for meetings
and events, 1971–76

pristine single-cell organism metamorphosing into cultures, cities, ethical imperatives, the sciences, the arts: volitional adaptation. Self-creation: the art of living?

A critical level of complexity and bonding has to be present to trigger volition. The whole spatial sequence, a nanobiotechnology, is a simultaneity of miniaturization, complexity, volition, *religare,* and automation: the presence of life.

There are volitional bundles called rabbits, volitional bundles called "lilies of the field," volitional bundles called dancers, scientists, lunatics, and so on. Volition is the faculty common to all. The drive generated within each bundle has another faculty in common, *religare*: the bonding faculty, the faculty of love in its most rudimentary nature.

Why, in a reality as vast as the cosmos, does the living phenomenon have to occur only as phenomenal bundles of miniaturization and complexity? Life is not separable from the nanobiotechnology of its own makeup. The powerhouse of life is in the immensely small and enormously complex bundles, literally bundles of stardust. Life is a maniacally miniaturized and maniacally complex packaging of atomic and subatomic stuff coming in countless variations, organisms, self-creating volitional "religature."

In exercising volition, space is very finicky about selecting its geometries; it is religiously going after them, corralling them into organism. And voilà, life is: it is operational and is volition-religion creating itself.

The urban effect as universal effect is the transformation of mineral matter into mind via the potentially unlimited power of complexification and miniaturization. Such is the case of organisms: single, composite, associative. In eschatological terms, the upper limit of the process could be the concluded esthetogenesis in a cosmic seed, the Omega Seed.

Soleri, at left, shaping the silt-cast form for the concrete roof of the Institute of American Indian Arts outdoor theater in Santa Fe, 1966

The Concept of Arcology

The arcology concept proposes a highly integrated and compact three-dimensional urban form that pursues the opposite of urban sprawl, with its inherently wasteful consumption of land, energy, and time, tending to isolate people from each other and community life. In an arcology, the built environment and the living processes of the inhabitants interact as organs, tissues, and cells do in a highly evolved organism. This means that multiple systems work together, coordinated and integrated to minimize waste while maximizing efficient circulation of people and resources, employing multiuse structures, and exploiting solar orientation for lighting, heating, cooling, food production, and esthetic impact.

The essential problem I am confronting is the present design of cities only a few stories high, stretching outward in unwieldy sprawl for kilometers. As a result, they literally transform the earth, turning farmland into parking lots and wasting enormous amounts of time and energy transporting people, goods, and services over their expanses. My proposition is urban implosion rather than explosion. The city must cohere with the guidelines of the evolution of life. These are self-containment, sophisticated logistics, reduction of waste (the lean process), interaction with the "outer" world, richness of processes, self-reliance, and the generation of an inner light, the urban persona.

We have been decoupling the urban from the logistical (transportation). As long as we persist in hyperconsumption mode and automobile supremacy, this conflict has no solution. It is a simple fact of physics (transportation) and hyperphysics (urban effect). Every adult with a minimal understanding of physics in his or her brain knows (or better hurry up and know) that reduction of consumption and increase of three-dimensionality—a multistory habitat—offer the only alternatives to urban sprawl. The rest is pure deleterious delusion, the virtue of which is to fill the pockets of attorneys, politicos, builders, utility companies, and developers.

The morphology of the tree, namely the proximity of the leaves to the logistical network of the branches, is an analogy for the swiftness and economy that our systems try to emulate to no avail. In the lean construct of an organism, each cell of the body is fed and cleansed by astounding symmetrical networks of arteries and veins. Trillions of cells are kept living and working by the gossamer reticulum of an inimitable delivery-retrieval system. Our monstrous multitudes of automobiles, soon over six billion (the American dream), will never achieve even a pale approximation of the logistical perfection of any organism. Furthermore, a culture based on the car leads to the diaspora of habitat, inevitably segregating people and stifling true novelty, the synergy of culture and civilization.

Complexity is a worthwhile goal in planning and building cities because organisms at all levels of evolution are masterworks of complexity indissolubly tied to miniaturization. A society made up of complex individuals is a society defining ever more intricate synergies, as we all know when surveying our lives. What is needed is not a Disneylike simulation or an arcadia but a movement into the complex, self-clustering, environmentally coherent towns and cities we could invent if we put ourselves to it.

Self-Creating Reality

The big bang is the birth of space, a convulsion that could also be the origin of the cosmos if not of reality itself. The big bang birth is the ongoing event that we earthlings measure in fourteen or so eons, evidently according to our way of measuring. We have no way of seeing the big bang in its early youth or in its old age. Being more, far more, acquainted with reality could allow us a way to measure the entropy drift and have some approximation of a possible (probable?) end of the big bang, its self-generation and self-creation, the unstoppable metamorphosis of itself, space in action.

If the big bang is the birth of space, then space itself and its powerful transformism are what we can call the generating and creating presence, creative of everything without exception. The inscrutable presence that reality is has its moment or point of genesis in the big bang, the "explosion" of presence, the cosmos. The vastness of the big bang is the greatest mystery imaginable. The mystery of presence "taking over" nonpresence—a poor manner of speaking because nonpresence, unspeakable as it is, is not worth mentioning.

Assuming the big bang to be the howness of its presence, and endorsing the notion that the first hiatus of the big bang to be the "separation" of presence from an ineffable nonpresence, then the big bang is reality in progress, and we as everything else are the big bang in progress, members of its inscrutable speed-of-light journey. Philosophers are trying to make sense of reality. I, in my bottomless naivety, am trying to remind them they are dealing with the big bang, nothing less; nor could they deal with anything more. "More" than the big bang has probably never existed.

Center for Advanced Studies,
part of the Mesa City project,
a city designed for two million
inhabitants, 1956–64

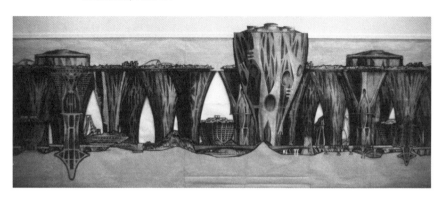

The most remote influence is the most pervasive.
Rather, the most pervasive is the most remote. Or rather
still, the sun belongs to the most remote sphere of
influence, yet is not only pervasive but invasive: it is the
indefatigable cogenerator of consciousness.

One can state unequivocally that there is no possibility
for consciousness to exist and operate in the absence
of organisms that are the epitome of a prodigious
degree of complexity made possible by an extravagant
degree of miniaturization: complexity so prodigious and
miniaturization so extravagant as to engender in organisms
the phenomenon of duration that enters synergetically into
the evolutionary advancement of the organisms themselves.

Howness is the way space reconfigures itself.
Miniaturization is the most economic, frugal way of
howness. Complexity is the rich content of such economy.
Complexity and miniaturization are inseparable, and they
are a take-it-or-leave-it proposition. To take it means to be
with and for life. To leave it means to be with and for death.
It is that pure and simple.

As there is no life without MCD, so there is no life without robotization, the automatism born from all the steps taken toward greater miniaturization-complexity. A bug is a "will" on autopilot just as a human is; the difference is in the degree of miniaturization-complexity undergirded by robotization.

As mass-energy is unrelentingly stirred by space-time in ways that generate more and more information-knowledge (complexity) contained in less and less space-time (miniaturization), reality witnesses the mineral memory at first, then the genetic memory, and finally the cultural memory. Duration is taking hold, in the sense that the past sees more and more fragments of itself being relived, being remembered.

"Form follows function" is a planetary lie. The plant was not a function in search of a form, life in search of housing. The plant was forming itself, still is, after four eons or so of labor time. Of successive pre-organic forms, a singular one triggered life (volition) in the function-follows-form manner. The form was there; the function generated from it. What was the case then is the case now, even if in a somewhat camouflaged sequence, since within the form acquiring new functions there is a blurring of which is which.

The brain is the organ that best exemplifies the axiom. It is a hyperlean performance of space able to reach into the most unpredictable heights of awareness and performance. We are told that up until now the form-instrument has a lot of "rentable space" in a sort of anticipatory idleness. Anticipation of feats yet to come, a form at the ready for millennia, a redundance of as-yet-not-occupied space: all the functions to be (function follows form).

Why cannot a brain be as massive and heavy as a city block? Because space and time are obstacles to the information-response circuitry. No miniaturization, no brain; no brain, no mind; no mind, no consciousness; no consciousness, no Love Project [see final section, below]. Effective minimization of space-time is needed for mass-energy to fully "display" itself, to act. Here is the ultimate dilemma. And the ultimate tragedy. All this points to the imperative of the urban effect.

At this very moment while your brain-mind works at absorbing or disregarding my words, you are the radiant demonstration of the utter certainty of complexity-miniaturization. Your gray matter is an astonishing fireworks of MCD in action. And our brain-minds are probably only the crude forerunners of immensely more lively and radiant things to come. A brain is not just a compact milieu, it is a miniaturized milieu.

These three distinct but inseparable agencies—miniaturization, complexity, duration—have not been merely instrumental but indeed causal for the evolution of the organic. Life is applied economy: MCD. To recognize their indivisibility, whose synergetic virtue surpasses any other, should cause a paradigm shift in the evolution of our thinking. It is providential that MCD points unambiguously at the resolution of our environmental dilemma and does so from the very center of our ethical-equity quandary.

Model of a dam with terraced greenhouses, part of the Two Suns Arcology project, exhibited at the Xerox Square Exhibit Center in Rochester, New York, 1976

The Lean Alternative

It happens that the historical moment in which we live is desperately in need of leanness because our species has, in *Homo faber*, an irresistible motivation toward transforming the environment in favor of comfort, security, and happiness, but lacking the knowledge, sense of context, sense of equity, wisdom, determination, and the cosmic awareness for a life transcending the "law of the jungle." *Homo sapiens* is a gifted animal but not an innocent one. He is an opportunist loaded with idiosyncratic faculties, not always amiable, and often obscuring the nobility of his better self.

The industriousness of *Homo faber,* exemplified in the Industrial Revolution, has produced the magic of materialism unlimited. We are taken by it because one dimension of man is opportunistic, signifying the transposition of the law of the jungle—effective, innocent, and ethically mute—into the human field: "If you can get away with it, go at it" is the maxim of busybody man, *Homo faber*.

The lean alternative is an attempt to reformulate the materialistic tide into a considered balance, where production, consumption, and worth form a balancing act, a graceful trinity working on the basis and inspiration of knowledge, learning, and transcendence. The lean alternative resonates with the lean hypothesis, finding the grace in leanness of means to achieve coherence and harmony in ends.

Any nonlean approach would be a planetary curse if extended to a projected ten billion people. This is not abstract thinking. This is hardcore realism for a human phenomenon that has not yet found a realistic response to the logistic-based nature of its species' development.

Transportation is fundamental, from the human body's circulatory system to the collective circulatory systems of our communal habitat. Yet we practically live our lives as if we were the stuff of angels, liberated (redeemed?) from subjection to gravity and other givens of planetary reality. We are in the process of setting up an absurd landscape—exurbia—supported by a litany of wrong logistical systems that are unsustainable.

The triumphal technological march of *Homo faber* is overloading the poorly designed arterial and venous logistical networks we have naively embraced. The suburban logistical network is sclerotic, and worse, doomed. In order to remain marginally viable, the life of the "organism" becomes grotesque. An aerial view of exurban diaspora evidences that grotesque, monotonous, shallow, delusional life. It is un-*civil*-ized—that is, deprived of *civitas,* the city—but serves well the production, consumption, segregation, waste, and pollution cycles of rampant, rapacious capitalism.

Here the word *reformulation*—to form again—refers to the imperative to reformulate intentions that, per se, are rapacious, no longer coherent, and constitute a race into capriciousness, self-contradiction, inequity, destruction, collapse, nemesis.

The Western formula has perhaps hit the zenith of unconditional materialism. Logistical paralysis is just one of the afflictions of the American landscape imposed by the antiurban diaspora. To attempt to reform this landscape is an exercise in too little too late. Mere reform falls short of the task of facing and coping with the new conditions generated by our industriousness, given that it is mostly an attempt to improve what exists, producing only a better kind of wrongness. Reform will not effect sufficient transformation because it works at improving the wrong

Ellis Island and Manhattan
density sketches by
twenty-seven-year-old Soleri
en route to Taliesin, 1946

thing and thus moves toward a predictable dead end.
In this context, the choice of our leaders is most critical.
One has reasons for panic and sadness for the low grade
of our present leaders.

Two alternatives are: do more with less, or do less with
more. Lean society is a realistic proposition that could
embrace have and have-not alike. It is evolutionarily more
coherent than the hyperconsumption society. Evolution

might well be poised for an unparalleled acceleration, courtesy of learning and doing's new technologies. Though we are approaching the threshold of being able to provide food, shelter, and education for all people, we are immensely far from achieving anything like universal equity in distribution of such resources.

The lean alternative is not local, regional, or national in scope; it responds to a transnational need faced by rich and poor nations alike. It is instrumental because it advocates the pursuit of equity by establishing a habitat that encourages coherence with the most valuable inclination of our species: the optimization of mind via the optimization of our physical presence on the planet.

A network has to be developed that intentionally works toward the maintenance and development of what I call a lean culture, a culture sheltered and sustained by urban systems caring for the urban effect's richness and paying great attention to logistics of the life contained therein.

The conversion of hyperconsumerism into leanness needs to be physiological, psychological, and environmental. One out of three will not work, nor will two out of three. This conversion is not for people of lukewarm persuasion. It needs to reach a threshold of satisfying commitment or it wobbles and collapses. To be or to become of the lean persuasion is worth a lifetime of "financial anguish."

The lean habitat lessens dependence on massive injections of appliances, furnishings, equipment, gadgetries, and the enchantment of buying for the sake of buying, while two billion people are deprived of food, shelter, and dignity. Squalor does not just imply an impoverished, dilapidated physical place. Squalor resides also in the most opulent environs, where human dignity is trashed. Whereas we work assiduously to solve technical dysfunction when it occurs, we too easily go along with ethical dysfunction. Even when the dysfunction is out of "ignorance," this does not excuse the specific case, but merely obfuscates its causes.

Ground Village, part of the
Mesa City project, 1956–64

Esthetogenesis

I have been working on a hypothesis that proposes for reality a possible if remote conclusion into grace. The self-revelation of reality to itself: an *esthetogenesis*.

Esthetogenesis is a process generating a reality in which all components, besides being the means to achieving self-revelation, are also ends unto themselves, the very meaning of self-revelation. Esthetogenesis describes a state of grace that only consciousness, or some equivalent of it, can generate through evolution.

The esthetic light has to be created, and we are part of this creational process. The light is slowly being generated. By what? By consciousness. There is no mandate. There is no one telling you "You shall do this and you shall not do that," and so on. We create our conditions in darkness. And the darkness is with us until the possible final moment when the light has been created. The beauty would be that, in the end, you find out that you as a means have become the end, because you are an integral part of the end. We will, of course, all of us die before getting there. But we belong to something greater that is trying to get there by way of our efforts.

Where does the notion of beauty come from? At the very bottom, fitness—that is, the survival virtue—ought to be the secure gateway to beauty. But it does not seem to be. *Anthropos* sees not beauty in bacteria, slugs, cockroaches, crocodiles, hyenas, and the like. *Anthropos* has ambivalence toward its own beauty. The Stone Age goddess is pretty ugly, we say and maintain.

The aesthetic belongs to a different domain. The beautiful and the aesthetic have not much in common. What keeps them apart is the self-awareness of the human body-brain. Think of how "serene" is the inside of a jellyfish as compared with the "messy" inside of a person. Complexity carries its own price tag.

Any medusa of the ocean (jellyfish) is pure beauty in motion, and all specs of the animal are strictly functional. No trace of the aesthetic there, because there is no trace of transcendence in the animal. The animal is a perpetuation factory and involuntarily sings to the world.

There is no such thing as the esthetic per se, just as, for instance, there is no such thing as time per se. But while there are esthetic objectifications, time has no such thing; it is nonexistent. Both are contingent upon the stuff of reality: space reconfiguring itself. It can reconfigure itself in a sonnet, in a cathedral, in an image, in a black hole. Of all space configurations, though, the esthetic is only there where a mind has filtered the other objects through its anguish, coloring its becoming, and when such filtering converts the idiosyncratic into the "universal."

The maker and the beholder of the esthetic are contextual "antennas" detecting a not-yet-existent condition of grace. They are the receivers of that which could eventually be. In this, they transfigure human anguish into the transhuman esthetic. They can do this only by generating esthetic objects.

Silhouette photo of Hexahedron arcology, a plexiglass model exhibited at the Corcoran Gallery, 1970

From the big bang on, reality has been "factualizing" itself, presence after presence, and historically-evolutionarily documenting itself inscrutably as ever. As interpreters of it, as coauthors of it, we can carry on its understanding by way of "as if" conjecturing.

To my thinking, any proposition referring to a divine power is fictional because I do not think a god of any sort has ever existed. Consequently, the highly sophisticated mental elaboration of theologians, philosophers, historians, and thinkers of religion in general are concerned with nonpresences: God or gods.

My conjecturing takes all of those often noble exertions as products of dramaturgical humanity, that is, esthetic expressions, as are poems, plays, ballets, musical compositions, theatrical pieces, books, films, paintings, sculpture, architecture, and so on. The esthetic is always an intentional fiction. Michelangelo's Moses is not a flesh-and-bone presence; it is a large chunk of marble that Michelangelo vivified with his genius.

The theological synthesis occurs in the esthetic mode, its "true" field of endeavor: the monumental presence of the theological is in the poetry of its "holy" scriptures, from the most sanguine to the most elegiac, in its dramas, theaters, rituals, processions, chapels, churches, cathedrals, sculptures, paintings, murals, frescoes, manuscripts, sanctuaries, crucifixions.

Of the numberless hypotheses, conjectures, and dogmas manifesting the genius of the uniquely self-aware organisms that we are, fiction is intrinsic to the evolutionary process. Among the many fictions, I focus on two: the theological fiction and the esthetic fiction. The theological fiction has a history of transcending events in which gods are invented, exalted, betrayed, and forgotten. A potpourri of dogma, bloodshed, capriciousness, cruelty, anguish, exultation,

Soleri discussing Mesa City's
Ground Village scroll with workshop
participants in the Barrel Vaults
drafting studio at Cosanti, late 1960s

and exaltation; a monumental temple touching the cosmos and its evolution. A true process of transcendence that in its own pride denies its fictional nature.

The esthetic fiction, fully aware of its own make-believes, produces monuments and objects of often supreme energy and grace. The fiction that is the block of marble carved into Moses by Michelangelo is the esthetic in process of transcending all givens, organisms and institutions included: an anti-entropic evolutionary manifestation fitting, by the way, my definition of leanness.

The only possible liberation from idolatry is the reformulation of the whole theological realm into the esthetic realm. It is time for the equivocation to end and for us to marry these two fictions imbuing hominid history—the theological fiction and the esthetic fiction. By so doing, humanity may enter a new evolutionary reality—as it needs to—to remain true to its own virtue

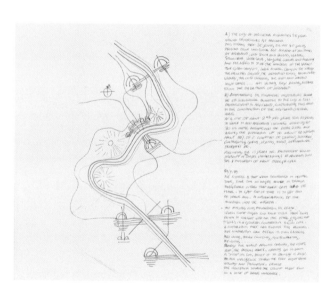

Early proto–Lean Linear Arterial City sketch, part of the Two Suns Arcology project, 1989

of self-creation. Together they are the unique and cosmic power of self-aware *Homo faber–Homo sapiens–Homo amor*

The theological-esthetic split has probably been an evolutionary diversion and is in need of mending. It is difficult for us, conservative as all organisms are, to develop a new language expressive of the two fictions in a universal-cosmic geometry. But if the big bang signifies anything, that fullest imaginable potential is what it might become: the big bang of grace.

To outgrow the failings of the present is the inescapable responsibility of that very same present, with its complement of joy and suffering. That is the context and content of self-creation. The inadequacy of the flesh that we all agree upon does not demand its demise, but a reformulation of its nature. Evolution from the big bang on demands reformulations in droves, the very glory and cross of self-creation.

Sketch combining Hyper-Building and Urban Ribbon, a proto–Lean Linear Arterial City concept, September 1996

The Love Project

Love is a reality for *Homo sapiens* because for four eons or so on this planet the triadic paradigm of miniaturization-complexity-duration has been at work. And what a masterpiece! What sparks out and radiates from such masterpiece is consciousness and mind. Where MCD is not implemented, the nature of reality remains coarse, blind, perhaps meaningless, and certainly below the threshold of love and compassion, of self-recognition. That means that it is incapable of self-consciousness.

It's one thing to propose the universe as indifferent to life in general and to mankind in particular. It's another thing altogether to propose that the universe is meaningless and that a meaning might eventually be generated via awareness, and more so by self-awareness, via the hominids in this solar system. At the present evolutionary stage, the last proposition sounds ludicrous and it might well be. The planet itself, in size and energy, is almost a zero in the universal scale of things. Life on it is a smudge.

Life drifts for eons in the megacosmic potpourri, a newcomer full of arrogance and dread. Will it take hold? And if it did, could it take command? How remote a prospect.

The fate of the big bang is to cool itself to zero degrees, into a frozen death-presence. To escape entropy would necessitate that space geometries be free of all those geometries we call energy. Until now, we have known of only a geometry so equipped, bound toward the absolute zero temperature of a frozen reality, a frozen cosmic geometry, a timeless death. Still a presence or the absence of presence? Adieu "music of the spheres."

Anguish is at the core of life, not joy. The noble task of the mind emerging within reality is not to dislodge anguish in order to instill joy but rather to transfigure anguish, the suffering of the flesh, and transform becoming into grace. The grace of stepping into a reality (that is, the creation of a reality) finally imbues meaning into the *what*, and into the *why* of such whatness. It forecasts a reality constituted of truly astonishing and glorious stuff. Until now, some ninety percent of life has been aborted or destroyed before it could break into significance. We have to accept that suffering and anguish are a large portion of what we are made of. But instead, the cart of animism is put in front of the horses, despair and hope, in order to obscure and deny their black hole. Reality is too vast, too indifferent, and too dumb to be moved by any moan of an infinitesimal "smudge" of life and consciousness.

If there is any hope for grasping and rejoicing in reality, the hope resides in the knowledge slowly developing in the species and the awe such knowledge generates in our body-brain: the supreme grace and beauty germinating from self-creation after eons of the self-generation of a lifeless and mindless cosmos.

In searching for self-revelation, reality must adapt and adopt whatever *how* is suited for the purpose. Reality can do that only when mind emerges from it and mind begins to want and to discriminate, to choose. Why is the esthetic at the core of it? Because the mind needs to pluck out of its feverish chase some incorruptible nugget of finality, of conclusiveness. It is unavoidable that the makeup of such practice is the distillation of the fundamental anguish, intrinsic to the condition of man, into the incorruptible esthetic object, which is the documentation of it.

The pristine cosmos, dumb and fierce, alien to grace at the core, can become lovable and loving only by way of a battery of transcendences, each one more momentous than the preceding. Thus the urban effect becomes a "religious stress" attempting the transfiguration of matter (space), the genesis of a divine totalizing grace.

It is up to the human brain-mind in its hunger for grace and equity to carry MCD to the fullest potential, perhaps to an unimaginable and immensely remote possibility, perhaps to a big crunch point of pure self-knowing, symmetric to the big bang point of pure mass-energy and space-time (the inseparable agents then in a nascent stage).

One can hypothesize a point in the future when time is totally consumed into duration. This would be the Omega Seed, the seed of the cosmos—symmetrical and opposite to the big atom of the original big bang—which would be radiant of all that has been its genesis. Thus it would be a state of total recall; that is, of total resurrection. The "resurrected" then will not be personae because they will be the quivering of reality that has found its significance and its own grace, no longer spatial but durational.

Omega is not an attractor because it does not exist. The Omega Point of Pierre Teilhard de Chardin, for instance, is at most an anticipation: the meaninglessness of the origin anticipating meaningfulness—a word game for the "time" being. As metamorphosing space ourselves, there is no way we can auto-define ourselves, hence no way we can define space. We are creating it with our becoming and we are in good company: reality, self-creation in search of itself.

The noble infinitesimal blur of life capped by the human experience is in the shape of a question mark, clamoring for everlastingness.

My infant God is a creational process with no inevitability associated with its emergent journey. The odds that it will mature and prevail are dismal, yet it remains the only hope for the cosmic "know thyself," the Omega Seed. At the end of the twentieth century,

I would redefine spirit as emerging self-awareness and discard the traditional primordial conception of spirit as an animistic delusion. If there is no inception and evolution of spirit—no embryology of spirit, birth of spirit, infancy of spirit, maturity of spirit, or transcendence of spirit—then the whole dynamic of creating God is meaningless. God the Creator is left in its horrendous determinism.

The Omega Seed event is the extreme instance of miniaturization-complexity-duration, within which, in a nullified space-time, the whole cosmic experience from beginning to end, big bang to big crunch, is revealed to itself: pure total being.

Now we experience love personally, locally, and parochially. Then, in the Omega Seed, love would be experienced catholically, cosmically, and conclusively. This would be space's exhaustion into the know-thyself mantra of the cosmos. The cosmos, the geometry to end all geometries.

Soleri drawing a section of Arcosanti 2000 (for 2,000 inhabitants) in his Arcosanti studio with triangular rulers and charcoal, ca. 1992

A Conversation with Paolo Soleri

Interviewed by Lissa McCullough, March 2011.

Paolo, for decades you have been elaborating a conceptual framework in your notebooks. Why did you turn to conceptual writing, and how essential is it to your work as an architect?

The movie *The King's Speech*, royalty aside, brought me back to my personal battle with communication. Quite a bit of my solitary character was formed because heavy stuttering kept me from the normal exchanges so important to human life and made schooling a sort of daily trial. Memorizing—very difficult for my brain—was a frustration since the recital via memory was so difficult. The escape? Monologuing. Handwriting is the recording of those bits of monologuing I thought to be useful to me and others.

The almost instantaneous cessation of my stuttering, I guess, was due to the use of French during my residence for over a year in Grenoble. I am sure various physiological-psychological factors were present, but it certainly was a brusque change of landscape between Grenoble Art Lyceum and Turin Polytechnic.

When asked about your emphasis on writing, you replied, "Well, I have a different way of thinking about architecture." How would you characterize this difference?

Part of the architectural profession involves talking to the many sides of the profession itself, knowing well that the silence of monologuing is the rule. Architecture is part of the self-creation our brains excel in, now and in the past. The construction of shelter is one of the early features distinguishing *Homo faber* from paleo hominids. A few epochs later, we are still at it, and history is full of marvels.

One extraordinary example: no self-respecting town or city in the United States lacks the Buonarroti dome. Think of how one single person from Florence produced the object in question that generated Buonarroti style that led to the millions of tons of stone and marble constructions. Architecture is the *hows* of space, its own geometries organized to serve the minutia of *Homo sapiens*. From mud, stone, and vegetation to steel and exotic materials, architecture has participated in the reformulation of cultures.

Your writings lament the gigantism generated by the, as you call it, "automobile-industrial-financial complex"—a planetary plague afflicting the urban fabric. How would you contrast this gigantism with the miniaturization you embrace? What does it take to reverse gigantism into a miniaturizing process?

Miniaturization is the shortening of distance between the components of an event: space becoming scarce. A point is absence of space. The cosmos (that is, the big bang in action) is the megapresence of space. *I* am not embracing miniaturization; I and all organisms *are* miniaturization in action. Gigantism is a separator, as evolution demonstrates. Death itself is the conclusive separator.

Marginalizing the car, which is *causa prima* of urban gigantism, is a necessary step toward the implosion of our presence on the planet. The implosion pursued by the urban effect: the *me*'s transcending into the *us*, the phenomenon of human culture by now emerging as an evolutionary presence.

The ratio of the two-hundred-pound biomass of a human person and the two- to three-ton mass of the car per se denounces the critical discrepancy between means and aims. The consumption of energy to pursue the aim is the second aspect of car gigantism. The space occupied by the idle car is the third. The fourth, and most gigantic, is the production of the car and the enormous, gigantic, technological, distributive, financial, social, environmental ziggurat of the car. This is the price exacted from car-blessed societies that have elevated it to the status of icon, and now often idol. And evolutionary stresses like this one don't know borders.

You have written that we and other animals are the real "automobiles"—the car is not a true auto-mobile. What do you mean?

"Automobile" is a semantic slip of the tongue since all organisms are automobiles, which the car definitely is not. Auto-mobile refers to an innerness generating mobility. Ask the car where any innerness resides in it. In the starter key? The arcane secrecy of the organism's volition is the answer. All organisms are auto-mobiles. The nonorganism that is the car doesn't have that faculty. It is a machine; it has never been an organism. In Italy, the car is *la macchina*, the machine. It does not possess the faculty of mobility. It is externally ordained automation.

Speaking of mobility, your earliest published design, The Beast, was a bridge, and you have designed many bridges since. Recently your focus has been the Lean Linear Arterial City. Is there a morphological link between your bridges and Lean Linear?

The link is simple and ever present: logistics. My insistence on using the term *arterial* in the Lean Linear design is that a generous availability of logistics is as imperative in our infrastructural urban landscaping as it is in any organism.

In a way, the Lean Linear is a further sequence, a modulation, of bridges like the Ponte Vecchio in Florence, open for the business of life and cultures, a historical sequence texturing life's evolution.

> You describe suburban habitat as "storage" rather than architecture. Millions move through a series of isolating boxes daily: office cubicle, motor vehicle, home "storage" unit— not to mention the media box that is the household focal point. This way of life seems designed as an escape from urban social interactivity. How can a nation of box-dwellers and box-watchers be persuaded to come out of the box? Why should we? What is at stake?

The storage of hermit people in planned communities, generous in space, deprived of humanness, does not qualify as architecture. They belong to devolution, a storaging. So yes, it might be useful to distinguish architecture from shelter-storage, keeping in mind that architecture might nonetheless turn out to be a form of shelter for a large group. Megachurches, for instance, and emergency shelters can reach levels of excellence.

At stake is an either-or: either we can see ourselves as transient episodes in a process toward which we have no loyalty, viewing our morphological makeup as an accident among countless others, so that we take our episodes as they come, ignoring, for instance, the simple fact that our doing today is consequent upon yesterday's doing; or we can see ourselves as those same episodes in a process unavoidably "capturing" us—and justly so—if reality is an unbroken sequence of self-generating, self-creating episodes whose unique *causa prima* is the big bang, the "tremendous mystery" of presence. It seems that what I call the urban effect is the optimal locus for the singular transient episode of the persona to be invested and partake in the cosmic storm triggered by the big bang.

> *If suburban life is an evasion of urban sociality, is part of the problem that the logistical inefficiencies of our modern cities provide poor models for imagining the pleasures and rewards of the coherent city?*

I'm not abreast of what cities in other countries do, but in the United States, the primary reason might be cultural. The power of the city wasn't appreciated by the values of immigrants pursuing survival and rapid improvement at whatever price. A rich culture takes time, commitment, and self-discipline—and possibly delusion. The fast tempo of the United States has little patience. Somehow, the young America hasn't found time to grow up. The gun, now second in the marathon of idols after the car, testifies to its caveman nostalgia.

Perhaps the second reason for the unenviable condition of cities in the United States is that they have been victimized by the car. New York City is an exception because New Yorkers have no great regard for the intrusive, pollutant, costly twenty-first century idol and its paralyzing gigantism.

> *For Aristotle, the polis was constituted by its citizenry not its geography or its buildings. We who dwell in modern cities tend to imagine that geography and buildings represent the city. Your urban thinking seems to place an accent on the synergy between living process and built environment, is that a fair statement?*

Yes, to represent does not say to be; in that sense, the structural side of the city is representative. One could say it is the skeletal aspect of the culture, which in full flesh is a composite of personae coactive in producing the urban effect. *Synergy* is the right word. Aristotle was possibly not aware of the close interconnections binding (*religare*) all things in an avalanche of episodes that are apparently heterogeneous.

> *You distinguish between* Homo urbanus *and* Homo tributus, *urban humanity and tribal humanity, and clearly you stake your bet on* Homo urbanus. *Yet many urban thinkers, such as Jane Jacobs and Lewis Mumford, advocate recreating the forms and values of interpersonal village life in the midst of a megapolis in order to sustain the caring "human face" of the city. Care to comment?*

The tribal bias and the urban bias are critical postures in human becoming. There is a strong nostalgia for tribal culture, to reinvent it. This is an unperceived mutilation of *Homo urbanus*. Most of what we have now, the bulk of science and technology, the bulk of products, the bulk of civility and culture, are the deeds of *Homo urbanus*, not tribal humanity.

The ethnic vivaciousness of New York City makes Jane Jacobs and Lewis Mumford right, but when the sap of the city that sustains this life becomes precarious, the group ethnicities suffer and often die. The barbarism of street gangs is perhaps a consequence of the loss of the city as a living hyperorganism. The caring "human face" becomes a burlesque mask.

> *Lewis Mumford also warned that cities often have taken mere physical and economic expansion as a testimony to prosperity and culture, not realizing that disorganization—or incoherence— is as fatal for a city as for an organism. Do we need a rigorous "urban science" to study how cities evolve and devolve?*

Mumford perhaps overlooks the "rigorous" disorder of reality engaged in its own inscrutable folly in gestating the inception of passion-impregnated reason. Cities are not beds of roses; they are more of the procrustean beddings keeping personae prancing around and making cacophony into chorales. Cultures are elements of the rigor that such chorales are made of.

The notion that the city is a high-energy consumer, that it is ungreen, ignores the fact that it is in the city where *Homo sapiens–Homo amor* touches transcendence, where evolutionary self-creation takes place. The city is the greenest of all environments. The city is authoring the homosphere.

> Today's New York Times (March 15, 2011) reported on the evolutionary theory that the root of human achievement lies in our ability to cooperate, to make individuals subordinate their strong sense of self-interest to the interests of the group. Would you say that arcology theory is betting on the evolutionary potential of that human capacity?

Yes.

> Often your writings bear the tag line "What if?" which is almost a Soleri trademark. What do you mean by it?

We are a species that knows that it does not know enough to ignore the fathomless *if*-ness of our rationalization. It is a faculty of the brain to modulate in "as if" mode the otherwise inscrutable reality in which it is operating.

> You argue there are no givens, no truths, only working hypotheses in an open-ended evolutionary process of creation—

The truth is not a given; it is the trueness of the process enabling reality to surge, tiny bit by tiny bit, to higher manifestations. As, for instance, when a conjecture concerning a flat planet Earth gives way to a spherical body in the vast expanse of the cosmos, yet to be deciphered for its astounding complexity, still self-generating within an inscrutable reality. In this way, conjecturing concretizes into history. Myriad of those events are the collectively, "religiously" bonded effects in the evolutionary process. Among its other virtues, this process disposes of truth as the eternally given. In place of mummified Truth is the mercurial trueness of these evolutionary tsunamis.

> If reality is inscrutable, as you so often comment, this seems to imply that we all function as "architects" of reality in the way we perceive and act in an inscrutable world. Is that what you mean by self-creation—that we are, each of us, cocreating the world?

Yes we are, keeping in mind that at one appropriate dimension the bacteria are also creating while wriggling in the stale soup; self-creation cannot exclude any of the dimensions of reality, micro or macro, constituting every present. But the greatness of self-creation consists in the ever-present sophistication of its own selectivity. The past is the repository of this progression from the cosmic dust of the big bang to the splendid manifestations of the human mammal. We are architects when we build shelters. We are "architects" in the cosmic sense when we unavoidably employ our life as cocreator of incipient reality.

> Your August 2010 notebook contains an insight that struck you: "We are the big bang." What was that insight?

Drawing of Hyper-Building, a design
project solicited by a Japanese consortium
from participants Soleri, Rem Koolhaas,
and Nobuaki Furuya, 1996

Making a fool of myself via my ignorance, I still maintain that the big bang is the inconceivable birth of space: space and only space, incarnate in the endless play of its geometries, is the whole of self-creating reality. This "position" makes the big bang an ongoing evolutionary presence. Two cosmic processes: the big bang generating more and more space; evolution nested in the big bang creating itself. We do not depend on the big bang to carry on self-creation. We *are* the big bang carrying on self-creation. We are coauthors and enactors of the big bang "dusting" ourselves up within billions of years of our prehistory: fourteen or so billion years of authorship as performers and observers—a big, big, big deal! Suffering, joyful, coherent, incoherent, trivial, sublime—a cosmic particle.

My position is not reductionist; my position is minimalist. Nothing is or becomes outside the big bang. Each organism is the big bang in action, all of its thousands of billions of billions of molecules. We humans are self-creating in the company of countless other self-righteous volitional individuals with our self-agitating, anxious personalities.

> *You emphasize coherence in all domains. Is this a way of talking about a proclivity to connect and interrelate that is finally a way of talking about* love *objectively, without dredging up the sentimentality and subjectivity that word evokes? Is this the connection between your quest for coherence and the Love Project?*

It gives me real pleasure that you somehow voice my apparent detachment from the human conundrum by not using the term *love*, a word that has lost meaning through inflation, and see my "proclivity" as possibly "hyperlove," as that drive asserting a tendency, a seeking of cosmic novelty, thanks to the surging of life within the immense indifference of reality. "Hyper" points toward the transcending that seems to be most of the time hidden, soliciting what I call self-creation. This is where the imperative of leanness voices itself as coherence—and urges the "objective" take on love.

What do you intend by your distinction between the feasible *and the* desirable?

The desirable is that which is beyond immediate survival demands and naked opportunism. In that sense, desirability is the trigger to transcendence when by transcendence we mean evolutionary steps that the genetic imperative per se is unable to take, deprived as it is of reflective know-how and knowledge. Whereas the feasible is inseparable from technology—from *how* things are done—and is thus an agency present at the very onset of becoming, from the big bang onward the desirable is strictly a mental invention. Plants, animals, and minerals do not dwell in the desirability domain. Their domain is opportunistic, probabalistic, deterministic, is made of presentness and always innocent.

I maintain that my efforts are oriented toward the desirable. The feasibility of the desirable is dependent on the openness of the contextual present, and it is something out of my hands.

Commentators call you "visionary" because of the scale of your proposals, but they tend to ignore that most of your built projects have been utterly hands-on. Your direct involvement in building has emphasized the trial-and-error process. What does your accent on the "urban laboratory," on process rather than product, promise to deliver?

The point is, reality itself is quite probably and only process. If so, "products," as critically important as they are, become by-products. The substantivism of the by-product is always only secondary in the tsunami-like cosmic process ever sweeping away what came before. The promise, and the threat, is to try to find the right tsunami or else.

> Building an arcology would seem to depend on the advent of an economic-political system (or subsystem, like Arcosanti) dedicated to pursuing frugality, leanness, and equity. Do you imagine that you are addressing a posterity generations from now?

Process finds its origin in a multitude of remote pasts, so historical dates—in evolutionary terms—become almost arbitrary punctuations. The future can't tell because it has never existed. Only the present receding into the past exists. History, the past, will tell, and although the labeling will be different, the content, if worthy, will maintain its own substantiveness.

> Why do you think a very long-range view is essential to architectural practice in the present?

Long-term thinking is the only realistic thinking, coming as we do from cosmic dust. We are faces of this dust metamorphosing in the raging chaos to which we belong, inescapably but not deterministically (self-creation sees to that). Only this long, long genealogy is "for real" and we are impregnated by the whole sarabande of trillions of trillions of molecules full of volition and religiosity. Our immediate presents are soon to be lost as instances of remote pasts. It is up to our actions—thinking being one of those actions—to be present in those remote pasts as specks of consciousness that had an offering to give to that very same evolution we monologue about. We as individuals have a brief moment to be swept up to become aware cocreators along with the inscrutable big bang.

George Bernard Shaw condemned "man" as incapable of solving problems raised by anything more complicated than a village—and not being capable of managing even a village very brilliantly. My sense is you might agree with him. Despite the apparent optimism of your arcological proposals, you are not optimistic, just open to stunning surprises. Is that fair?

Fair up to a point. Fate is the boundary that any context piggybacks on. Fate moves with and within the moving of the boundaries. Formerly, it was fatal that polio would cripple. It ceases to be fatal in the postvaccination era. I always maintain that in the short-term I am a pessimist, but I am a convinced and dedicated long-term optimist. History and evolution are on my side—from big bang dust we come.

Soleri's Architecture in Contemporary Context

Marco Felici

Paolo Soleri plays an inconvenient role of great importance in the history of contemporary architecture, so much so that it has been difficult to categorize him historically without inquiring into his true meaning. In the historical mosaic, Soleri is usually identified at the intersection of the vertical temporal axis of organic architecture and the horizontal cultural axis of the radical avant-garde. Although these labels are more than justified, they are also insignificant compared to the full extent of Soleri's work and his interdisciplinary openness. Urban density, protection of undeveloped land, zero-impact cities—these are just some of his concepts, hastily labeled as utopian by zealous reactionaries, that have entered the consciousness of an entire generation of aspiring architects and have become the main expressions of contemporary sustainable design.

Certainly Soleri has not, to date, had a real opportunity to apply the full scale and importance of his ideas concerning the reformulation of human habitat—a proposal with which he has been consistently experimenting for half a century. He has not had a chance to do it directly, nor has he had the opportunity to create a real school of architecture that promotes this objective. Yet indirectly, the potential of his research has indeed been highly effective, as very few in the history of modern and contemporary architecture have generated as broad and lasting of a following as Soleri has, although the extent of his influence has yet to be fully grasped and understood.

Surpassing any limited identification with some of his works of great reputation, Soleri's architectural production, along with his philosophical constructs, has had a long and important evolution identifiable through various milestones. His work, fully in keeping with his explanation of the evolution of reality, is stratified in continuous cycles of deepening and consolidation. It is his habit to start back from positions previously gained and then explore myriad variations on that theme, thus creating the next step in representing his thought and architecture.

The deep-seated parallels between his theoretical concepts (such as the urban effect, the principle of MCD, the lean alternative, and reformulation) and his architectural designs (such as Cosmic Potentials, Arcology, the Two Suns Arcology, and the Lean Linear Arterial City) demand to be explored. In each of these works— or rather, in each cluster of work in relation to the research that produced them—one can detect an achievement in the way we think about architecture, and even more about human habitat in a natural context. These are achievements that Soleri carries out through projects and prototypes, seemingly visionary, but in fact pioneering: it is not a coincidence that the quick appellation of "visionary" gradually recalibrates as the actionable intent of these proposals permeates the minds of newly inspired designers.

How can such long and prolific research, Soleri's huge influence on the evolution of architectural thought, and the anomalous discrepancy between this patent relevance and his distance from architecture's star systems be explained? All these questions probably have a common answer, or rather, they have an answer

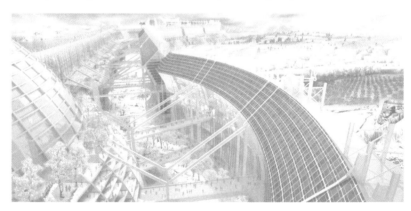

Overhead view of Lean Linear
Arterial Arcology set in winter
for a seasonal touch

intrinsic to the subject of the question itself. Isolation from the star system has allowed Soleri to develop an independent alternative to the dominant way of thinking, identifying and exploring solutions contingently uncomfortable until overturning the axioms on which the biggest problems of our time are based.

Isolation has also allowed the multivalent cultural diffusion of Soleri, keeping him out of the quagmire of trends. Having avoided the hurdle of immediate opposition—the petty defense of one's academic and professional position—Soleri's concepts have been well received and absorbed by everyone without fear of competition. The heroic extent of his research in radical architecture, moreover, ensures that Soleri continues to be a precedent and a source of inspiration rather than a rival or a stale teacher. And his precedent is far from static. As it continues to evolve it will provide new generations of young designers with ideas to absorb in their personal escape from academic teaching—ideas that they unconsciously keep stored away under their rationalist indoctrination until they reappear in their mature works. This has assured Soleri's continuing influence on the architectural scene, even if momentarily postponed by the time required for a generational turnover.

This is already quite evident in The Beast (1948), an early bridge project Soleri worked on as an apprentice to Frank Lloyd Wright, in which he surpassed the master, according to international critics, and which probably determined his departure from Taliesin. The bridge is a brilliant intuition on the potential of resistance by form, which has since influenced many acclaimed bridge designers. Soleri's significance becomes even more evident with his research into Cosmic Potentials, passive and active energy resources to be used in construction; begun during the 1940s, this research achieved international fame in 1949 with the completion and publication of the Dome House. But it was only in the 1970s, when the world energy crisis revealed the need to pay special attention to the topic of energy conservation, that the production of ecofriendly buildings began to spread, with the design of so-called bioclimatic buildings.

By this time, however, Soleri was already talking about Two Suns Arcologies, cities where bioenergetic criteria are applied at an urban scale. Not surprisingly, as noted by architectural critic Jeffrey Cook, the superstars of sustainable design have marked their training with visits to Soleri's projects in Arizona, and simple solutions already theorized in his Cosmic Potentials have become the shared common background of ecofriendly designers.

Today, the leitmotif of the latest theories of urban planning is the need for building density and the need for land protection by stopping and reversing urban sprawl. These are exactly the assumptions made by Soleri's *Arcology: The City in the Image of Man*, published by MIT Press in 1969. Arcological proposals provide testable, workable approaches to the intrinsic need to reduce automobile traffic, fuel consumption for seasonal air conditioning, waste of agricultural land, and isolation of people from each other. What Soleri illustrated in the 1960s and 70s is finally being actively applied some forty years later, although on a lesser scale of importance compared to the potential of the original idea.

And in the meantime Soleri is advancing further ahead. In succession to arcology and the lean alternative, reformulation is the new target toward which he is challenging us to think. His proposal for a reformulation in architecture now is embodied in the Lean Linear Arterial City, a linear three-dimensional arcology on a global scale, which develops all urban functions around international rail routes. Here people can live in an osmotic membrane between the urban center, the engine of all transactions, and the natural environment, agricultural or natural. The *sub*-urban area disappears because the linear urban center is always nearby; the car disappears because it is useless in the three-dimensional structure of the habitat; the warmongering oil dependence also disappears because energy is produced by the city itself; and finally, theology disappears because we enter a new phase of cosmogenic evolution in which human beings no longer need to look outside of physical reality to account for consciousness.

Soleri's Lean Alternative in the Developing World

Youngsoo Kim

Soleri defines leanness as "elegant frugality," and this commonly implies maximized efficiency. Frugality entails not only conservation of energy and materials but also the comprehensive recognition of environmental and social costs of consumption. Thoughtless consumption of material and energy is avoidable when the true cost of a design is understood thoroughly. By introducing the concept of a lean alternative, Soleri intends to render the invisible costs of any design product visible. Elegance can be introduced only when the quality of the design product is achieved through a process of pursuing frugality. In this sense, the pursuit of leanness could be adopted as a fundamental design principle for cities that are now under the pressure of relentless material and energy consumption.

Today, more than 50 percent of the world's population resides in urban areas, and this figure is expected to exceed 60 percent by 2030. Over the last century, the world urban population has risen drastically from 220 million to 3.2 billion. In the midst of this explosion of urbanization, more than 90 percent of urban growth will occur in developing countries such as China and India.[1] Currently, in China, more than 600 million people, or 44 percent of the entire Chinese population, are living in cities.[2] It is also projected that the migration trend from rural to urban areas will surpass 350 million people by 2030; China's urban population will exceed one billion people. To accommodate this rapid rural-to-urban migration, Chinese cities need to build more than five million buildings— equivalent to two hundred cities with a population of more than one million—over the next twenty years.[3] Rapid urban population growth is also leading developing countries toward dramatic increases in consumption of resources and energy and generation of pollution. Cities are causing more than three-quarters of global pollution and demanding three-quarters of the world's energy. Most of the highest-population cities, again, are located in the developing world.

Given these numbers, it is reasonable to assume that most energy and resource consumption and environmental pollution will be concentrated in the cities of the developing world. Therefore, what kind of urban growth model these cities pursue becomes critical with respect to energy usage and pollution control—not only for developing countries but also developed ones. Unfortunately, many of the cities in developing countries are looking at a model that relies on heavy consumption of energy and resources, leading to serious environmental and social challenges.

The automobile and its industry, which depend on limited fossil-fuel resources for their production and maintenance, have been the major driving force behind economic growth in the developed world, and are increasingly becoming so in the developing world. While the automobile has served as a key catalyst for the economy, it also is one of the main contributors to air pollution and suburban sprawl, promoting inefficient use of resources and energy in the city. In the United States, transportation is responsible for almost 30 percent of total greenhouse gas emissions, resulting in economic and social costs (such as health care) equivalent to three hundred billion dollars a year.[4] In the metropolitan area of Phoenix, where suburban sprawl is the greatest in the United States, 73 percent of residents commute alone by car while fewer than 4 percent use public transportation, bicycle, or walk. One result of this heavily car-dependent commuting pattern is manifested in poor air quality in the Phoenix area, which was ranked forty-seventh out of fifty metropolitan cities for air quality in the United States in a 2008 sustainability ranking.[5] The U.S. population constitutes less than 5 percent of the world population while consuming 21 percent of the world's energy; China, by comparison, constitutes 20 percent of the world population while consuming 16 percent of the world's energy.[6] If China were to consume the same energy per capita as the United

States, it would demand 84 percent of the world's energy and eventually exceed the limits of world energy production.

Thus, expanding Chinese cities put imperative pressure on the world. What should the urbanization model be for cities in the developing world? The Lean Linear Arterial City is Soleri's lean alternative for urban development and could suggest an answer to this question. In the Lean Linear proposal, which he has been formulating since 2004, there are two major principles that can be meaningful considerations for cities in the developing world.

The first is *proximity*. Soleri compares the circulation system in the city to the arterial system in the human body. The arterial system delivers required oxygen and nutrition to each part of the body and is critical to its survival and health. The current car-based city model promoting the freedom of mobility by maximizing individual vehicle use is causing arterial sclerosis. By removing people from the street and designing it for car traffic instead, the circulation system puts distance between people and impedes social contacts and civic activities in the city. The interrelations of circulation systems with multiuse residence, work, and recreational spaces in Lean Linear are designed to promote proximity between people in the city. Public transportation systems and pedestrian circulation systems are the backbones that support the movement of people.

The second is miniaturization. Vehicular roads are taking over the principles that govern both the structure and growth patterns of cities in the developing world. Wherever cars can reach, cities sprawl, regardless of the negative impact on the environment. By maximizing the density of human settlements, Lean Linear minimizes environmental impact. Development follows the planned circulation system with the maximum density that is allowed in different environmental conditions. Many studies have shown the inverse relation between population density and energy consumption. Annual gasoline use per capita in Houston is thirty times higher than that in Hong Kong while the urban density of Hong Kong is twelve times higher than that of Houston.[7] When density is doubled, for instance, driving declines 20–30 percent, which leads to substantial reduction of energy use in transportation.[8] As density increases, the form of the city becomes increasingly three-dimensional, minimizing its overall footprint as well.

The Lean Linear model aspires to forge a synergy between efficient movement systems and increased density. Soleri does not presume that the Lean Linear model is the ultimate solution for rapid urbanization in developing countries. He does, however, assert it as a potential alternative that can successfully address the key problems that emerging metropolises of the developing world are confronting, with the intent to reformulate and redress the logistical inefficiencies of the currently predominant development model.

Continuous array of Lean Linear urban modules depicting a development on higher ground in a coastal region

1   United Nations Population Fund, UNFPA State of World
     Population 2007: Unleashing the Potential of Urban
     Growth (New York: United Nations Population Fund,
     2007), http://www.unfpa.org/swp/2007/presskit/pdf/
     sowp2007_eng.pdf.

2   Lamia Kamal-Chaoui, Edward Leman, and Zhang
     Rufei, "Urban Trends and Policy in China" (working
     paper, Organization for Economic Co-operation and
     Development, 2009), 5–6.

3   McKinsey Global Institute, Preparing for China's Urban
     Billion (Shanghai: McKinsey & Company, 2009), 15–20.

4   Richard Rogers, Cities for a Small Planet (Boulder, CO:
     Westview, 1998), 38.

5   SustainLane, "SustainLane Presents: The 2008 US City
     Rankings," SustainLane website, http://www.sustain-
     lane.com/us-city-rankings.

6   Center for Sustainable Systems, U.S. Environmental
     Footprint Factsheet (Ann Arbor, MI: University of
     Michigan, 2009), http://css.snre.umich.edu/css_doc/
     CSS08-08.pdf.

7   Peter W. G. Newman and Jeffrey R. Kenworthy, Cities
     and Automobile Dependence: An International
     Sourcebook (Brookfield, VT: Gower Technical, 1989),
     388.

8   McKinsey Global Institute, Preparing for China's Urban
     Billion, 154.

Biographical Overview
Paolo Soleri

1919   Born June 21 in Turin, Italy.

1933–39   Attends the *École d'Art Industriel* in Grenoble, France, then Accademia Albertina delle Belle Arti in Turin.

1940–46   Student at Turin Polytechnic, graduates with highest honors. Arrives in New York City en route to an internship with Frank Lloyd Wright.

1947–48   Apprentice to Frank Lloyd Wright at Taliesin, Wisconsin. Travels to Taliesin West, Arizona. Designs The Beast.

1949   Design and construction of Dome House in Cave Creek, Arizona, with collaborator Mark Mills. Marries Colly Woods.

1950   Returns to Turin and builds Leoncino camper to move to Vietri sul Mare, where he works as a ceramicist.

1951–54   Birth of first daughter, Kristine. Design of Solimene Ceramics Factory in Vietri sul Mare. Returns to the United States with family.

1955   Moves to Paradise Valley, Arizona, and begins ceramics production. Executes first designs of Cosanti.

1956   Birth of second daughter, Daniela. Retail sales of ceramics and construction of Cosanti begin. Initial designs of Mesa City, 1957–62. Teaches courses at Arizona State University (ASU), including silt-casting techniques, while continuing work on Cosmic Potentials and Mesa City. Awarded two Graham Foundation grants (1957 and 1961). Further designs of bridges and dams, first designs of arcologies, including Babel IIA. First workshop at Cosanti.

1963   Associate Professor at ASU's College of Architecture. Awarded the American Institute of Architects award for craftsmanship.

1964–67   Design and construction of open-air theater for Institute of American Indian Arts in Santa Fe, New Mexico. More arcology drawings and models. Cosanti Foundation established. Receives Guggenheim Foundation grant to support completion of Mesa City (1964) and a second to formalize arcology designs (1967).

1968–69   Cosanti Foundation purchases 860 acres of land 60 miles to the north for construction of Arcosanti. *Arcology: The City in the Image of Man* is published by MIT Press.

1970   Arcosanti construction begins. Major exhibition hosted by the Corcoran Gallery of Art in Washington DC, The Architectural Vision of Paolo Soleri, attended by more than 100,000 visitors. The exhibit traveled to the Whitney Museum in New York and numerous other locations in years to come.

1971–74	Further construction of Arcosanti. More book publications. Becomes a U.S. citizen.
1975	Two Suns Arcology project and exhibit in Rochester, NY, sponsored by Xerox Corporation.
1976–80	Ongoing construction of Arcosanti. Multiple exhibits of recent work at museums and universities.
1981	Awarded gold medal for architecture at the World Architecture Biennial in Sofia, Bulgaria.
1982–85	Wife Colly dies in February 1982. Nominated member of the International Academy of Philosophy, Switzerland. Space for Peace designs and models. Silver medal for research and technique from the Académie d'Architecture in Paris (1984). More book publications.
1986–88	Design of the Cancer Center chapel at the University of Arizona Medical Center, Tempe. Conferences in Tokyo and Jerusalem. New bridge designs.
1989–92	Five annual Minds for History conferences at Arcosanti attended by diverse prominent figures such as Nobel-winning poet Czeslaw Milosz, feminist author Betty Friedan, composer John Cage, and scientists Stephen Jay Gould and Murray Gell-Mann. Exhibit of Ecological Minutiae at ASU. Soleri's Cities: Architecture for the Planet Earth and Beyond exhibition at Scottsdale Center of the Arts.
1996	Design of Glendale Community College amphitheater. Invited to design Hyper-Building by Japanese Hyper Building Research Committee, Tokyo (architects Rem Koolhaas and Nobuaki Furuya also invited). Nominated honorary member of the Royal Institute of British Architects.
1997	Design of Scottsdale pedestrian bridge. Icon exhibit at MoMA, San Francisco.
1998	Participated in traveling exhibit in Tokyo, São Paolo, Berlin, and Los Angeles.
2000	Awarded the Golden Lion award for lifetime achievement at the Venice Biennale. Graham Foundation grant for photo documentation of Soleri archive.
2002–04	Conference on Soleri at the Academy of Architecture in Mendrisio, Switzerland, and visit of Swiss architect Mario Botta to Arcosanti. Intensive Soleri workshops at IUAV in Venice, as well as in Rome and Naples. Monograph entitled Soleri: Architecture as Human Ecology by Antonietta Iolanda Lima appears in English. Receives Commendatore Ordine al Merito della Repubblica Italiana, an award conferred by the President of the Italian Republic to reward excellence in arts and sciences.

2005	Major exhibition in Rome and Naples, Soleri Retrospective: Ethics and Urban Inventiveness, with detailed full-color catalog (*Paolo Soleri: Etica e invenzione urbana*, compiled by Sandra Suatoni).
2006	Receives the Lifetime Achievement Award from Smithsonian Institution's Cooper-Hewitt National Design Museum, New York.
2009	Exhibition of Lean Linear Arterial City proposal at the Beijing Center for the Arts, including an eleven-meter illuminated Plexiglas scale model.
2010	Completion of the Paolo Soleri Pedestrian Bridge and Plaza in Scottsdale and exhibit on Soleri bridges at Scottsdale Museum of Contemporary Art.
2011	Conceives the Ecumene project, a cluster of ten cylindrical modules around a central cloister. Formally announces his retirement as president of Cosanti Foundation on July 14.

About the Authors

Marco Felici is an architect trained at La Sapienza University of Rome with a degree in civil engineering and a PhD in architecture and city planning. Since 2000, he has collaborated with Soleri on various research, design, and educational projects. In addition to overseeing the preconstruction design of Phase 5 of Arcosanti's East Crescent, he served on the planning committee for major Soleri exhibitions in Rome (2005) and Naples (2006). From 2003 to 2006, he coordinated Arcosanti workshops for architecture students in Venice, Rome, and Naples. Working in Rome since 1999 with his own architectural firm, atePi, he has taught at La Sapienza, Roma Tre University, and Venice Institute of Architecture (IUAV) and is author of the book *Architettura ipersostenibile* ([*Hypersustainable Architecture*], 2006) and dozens of contributions to Italian architecture journals such as *Exibart* and *Arch'it*, including several essays on Soleri's architecture.

Youngsoo Kim received a bachelor of science in architectural engineering at Sungkyunkwan University, Seoul, Korea, and undertook an internship with the Arcosanti Planning Department in 2005. In 2008, he completed joint master's and bachelor's degrees in architecture with a concentration in urban design at the University of Arizona. After graduation, he was invited by Soleri to continue working in the Arcosanti Planning Department, overseeing projects such as the Lean Linear Arterial City design proposal—part of the 3-D City and Future China exhibition sponsored by Beijing Center for the Arts—which was published in the center's exhibition catalog. Kim's professional intention is to translate Soleri's Lean Linear model into practical applications for urban planning in developing countries that are experiencing rapid urbanization. He has recently published a book, *Lean Linear City: Arterial Arcology*, in collaboration with Paolo Soleri and the Arcosanti Planning Department staff.

Lissa McCullough is an independent scholar trained in religious studies and philosophy who has worked with Soleri as his editor since 2005. After undergraduate studies at the University of California, Santa Cruz, McCullough completed a master's degree at Harvard University in 1989 and a doctorate at the University of Chicago in 1999. She is now based in Los Angeles, having previously taught the study of religion at New York University, Hanover College, and Muhlenberg College.

Illustration credits

Page 1, 10 top, 50, 57, 59, 65:
© Ivan Pintar

Page 8, 18 top:
© photo by Stewart Weiner

Page 10 middle, 27, 35, 38,
48, 53, 54–55:
© Cosanti Foundation

Page 10 bottom, 14, 22:
unknown photographer

Page 12:
Vera fotografia Omniafoto
Torino, rip. vietata

Page 13, 43:
© Alfonso Elia

Page 16–17:
© David DeGomez

Page 18 middle:
© Tomiaki Tamura

Page 18 bottom:
© Annette Del Zoppo

Page 24, 44:
© Colly Soleri

Page 28:
photo by Dwight Hooker,
Chicago, May 1971

Page 30–31:
© Chris Ohlinger

Page 32:
© Michael Brown

Page 36, 80, 82:
3-D renderings by Youngsoo
Kim

Page 40:
photo by Bob Libey

Page 60, 61:
© Yuki Yanagimoto

Page 66:
© Michel Sarda

Page 75:
Rendering by Tomiaki Tamura

Page 88–89:
3-D rendering by Youngsoo
Kim and Tomiaki Tamura